Goodnight Madison

Written by: Angie & Ben Buelow
Illustrated by: Lindsey Salzwedel

Published by Orange Hat Publishing 2019
ISBN 978-1-64538-079-5

www.orangehatpublishing.com

WiscKids Books
Exploring Wisconsin Together

We dedicate this book to our two boys Colin and Gunnar, who have heard countless Goodnight stories. We have accumulated a number of Goodnight books highlighting the places we've visited. What was missing was one that captured the greatness of the city our boys call home. We hope you and your children enjoy reading this book and sharing the magic of Madison!

Goodnight

Farmer's Market

and hot cheesy bread.

Goodnight

Overture Center

and songs in my head.

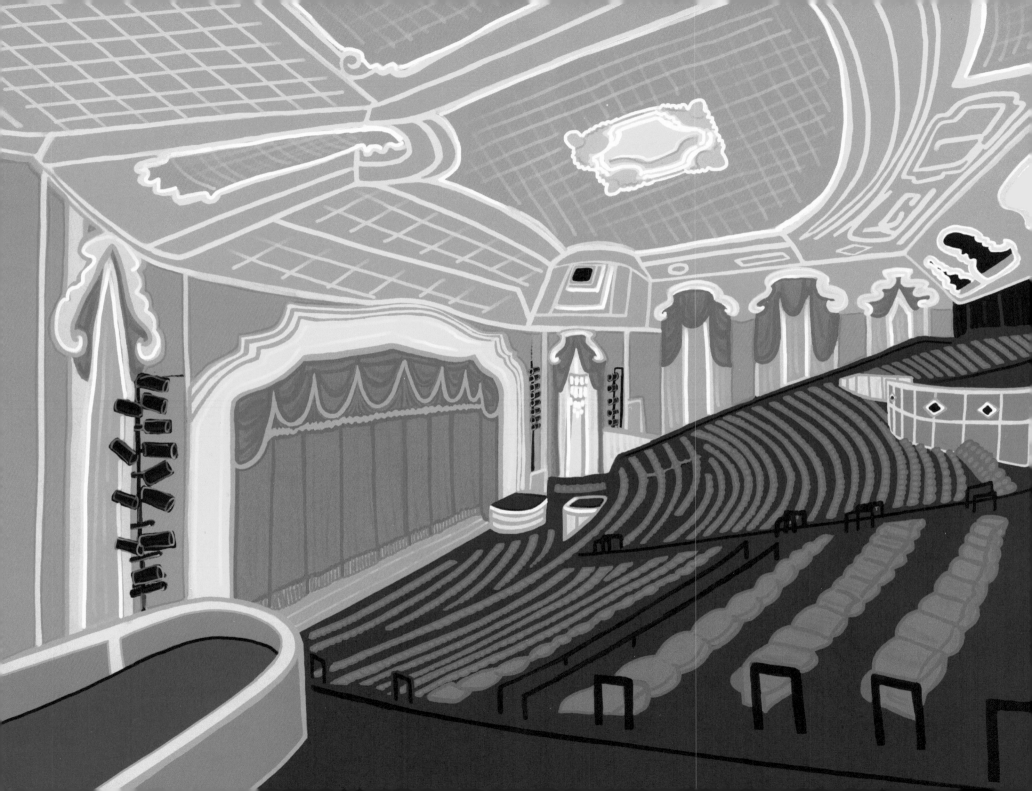

Goodnight

State Street,

all the stores and eats.

Goodnight

ice cream shops

and all tasty treats!

Goodnight to
the terrace
with your beautiful views.

Goodnight to
the chairs
and music too!

Goodnight

Camp Randall

and the Badgers that play.

Goodnight to

the fans

that jump around on game day!

Goodnight
Children's Museum
and Henry Vilas Zoo.

Goodnight to
the penguins
and polar bears too!

Goodnight

bike path

that loops around the lake.

Goodnight
craft brewers
and beers that they make.

Goodnight
Warner Park

where the

Mallards

play until dark.

Goodnight

Middleton, Fitchburg, and Verona.

Goodnight

Waunakee,
Sun Prairie,
and Monona.

Goodnight

pretty capitol

with your tall oak trees.

Goodnight to

the flags

that blow in the breeze.

Goodnight

university

with your books and knowledge.

I hope one day you're where I go

to college!

Goodnight

Madison.

I love you the best.

You're the most fun
city in the entire

Midwest!

Fun Facts About
Madison